I Am Montana

I Am Montana

Student Reflections
on Identity and Place

VOLUME 2

Edited by
>   Claire Compton
>   Dave Caserio

 Billings Bookstore Cooperative
Billings, Montana

Acknowledgments

We would like to thank all the individuals and organizations that have made this project possible: The National Endowment for the Humanities, Humanities Montana, and the Llewellyn Foundation; Wanda Morales, Claire Mikeson, Deni Oltrogge, and Marianne Bradley of the Billings Career Center; Montana Poet Laureates M.L. Smoker and Melissa Kwasny; Tami Haaland and Dave Caserio; Julie Schultz, Rosanna Buehl, and William Stearns from This House of Books; Free Verse teachers Nicole Gomez, Taylor White, Silas Miller, Lorna Buckingham, Olivia Round, Sam Dunnington; Nikki Zambon, Landen Beckner, Jesse Nee-Vogelman, Claire Compton, and Sam Hines; Michael Wade for proofreading assistance; and to all the poets in this anthology who have the courage to speak their truth.

Cover Art: "Untitled," Faith Smith

Cover Design and Interior Layout: Rosanna Buehl

Publisher   Billings Bookstore Cooperative
224 North Broadway, Billings, Montana 59101
(406) 534-1133
www.thishouseofbooks.com

Board Members

ISBN-13   978-0-578-87159-2

Contents

In Memoriam

Montana Poet Laureate

Marianne Bradley, Billings Career Center

9th Grade English Period 1

Wanda Morales, Billings Career Center

9th Grade English Period 3

Wanda Morales, Billings Career Center

9th Grade Honors English, Period 4

Free Verse

Instructors: Nicole Gomez, Taylor White, Silas Miller, Lorna Buckingham, Olivia Round, Sam Dunnington, Nikki Zambon, Landen Beckner, Jesse Nee-Vogelman, Claire Compton, and Sam Hines

Claire Mikeson, Billings Career Center
9th Grade English Period 4

Deni Oltrogge, Billings Career Center
9th Grade English Period 3

Montana Poet Laureate

Foreword

So much of Montana art and literature succumbs to familiar tropes, to pioneers and the rural West, to idyllic landscapes and the great outdoors. Although there may be remnants of truth in these tropes, they speak to a certain kind of story, a story written by those already empowered to speak, a story rooted in settler-colonialism.

I Am Montana aims to bring another kind of voice into Montana's literary legacy. Featuring work from students across our state, from high school classrooms to juvenile detention centers, this anthology aims to elevate young voices and voices from historically marginalized communities. The importance of this work echoes the shift we see happening across the country. Everywhere, people are recognizing that the voices we need to hear are not the ones we've amplified. Rather, they are the voices that have been silenced for generations.

When we began this project two years ago, we would have never imagined where our country would be today. Our home has changed. Our lives have changed. We are still growing, still learning how to fight the dual pandemics that plague our world—one viral, the other born of the legacy of white supremacy. We've seen how social isolation has renewed interest in the creative arts, how stories and poetry, live-streamed music, and virtual art galleries brought us together. Locked away from our families, friends, and lives, we discovered our shared humanity online and in books. However, we are again reminded of the question of access, the question of who gets to speak and who benefits from the narratives we share.

We hope the following pages offer an alternative, that they provide a platform for young voices to be heard, shared, and honored as vital pieces of the greater Montana narrative. We believe that through their work, we might come to find alternative ways of knowing this world, ways that go beyond common tropes to uncover the complexity and nuance of life in this state, in this country, in this moment of history.

Claire Compton, Executive Director of Free Verse

Foreword

Two words, two states of being, come to mind when I read again the poems in this book: uncertainty and resiliency. These young writers recognize, perhaps far too early, that life may not unfold as neatly as one imagines or expects. They face a list of ever-growing pressures, events, and conditions that contribute to the precarious nature of uncertainty–the shackle of imprisonment, the anxiety of familial dysfunction, issues of self-control, of personal behavior and actions, self-doubt and apprehension of the future, and of political and cultural forces beyond their control. All of this coming at an age where one is just beginning to embrace the possibilities of identity, of what one might be, could be, will be.

Yet there is that second condition: resiliency. And this in equal measure is also inherent in the poems of this anthology. Again and again, these young writers seek to mend what is broken and to make reliable what might be uncertain. They value kindness and empathy, hard work and personal honesty. There is wit and humor in these poems, and devotion to family and friendship, to self-knowledge, and to asking questions and seeking answers.

These tangled themes of uncertainty and resiliency were taken up by Montana Poet Laureates, Melissa Kwasny and M. L. Smoker who were able to visit and work with the 9th grade students at the Billings Career Center. Their positive impact upon the students was immeasurable and we are grateful for their time with us. Each graciously offered a poem for the anthology, which bookend the work of student writing. Here too are poems on the pliability and possibility of identity, and on the resiliency and rejuvenation of the human spirit.

We would like to honor, and remember, Cash Taylor, a 2019 graduate of Billings Senior High School, whose life was cut short in a tragic accident shortly after the publication of volume one of *I Am Montana*. His poem, "Best Memory Poem," was the final entry in the anthology. One cannot help but recognize and enjoy Cash's carefree, but cherished, description of growing up in Montana. One can also sense the unspoken story that sails beneath the surface of the poem. But whatever that story might be, it does not dampen the buoyant energy of the poem, or deny the resiliency and optimism of this young man's outlook. It is as if in the moment of looking backward upon himself, he is able to redirect his gaze forward into the future of what he might become, and to appreciate the gift of family and his place in the world. Cash Taylor's poem is made all the more poignant by his loss and it is fitting that we retain his memory in ours and that his poem be the opening poem of this year's anthology.

Dave Caserio, author, This Vanishing

In Memoriam
Cash Austin Taylor

March 12th, 2001–December 1st, 2019

Best Memory Poem

Cash Taylor

Growing up with all the toys we could think of
From Four Wheelers, Snowmobiles, Campers, ATVs,
Boating, Ice fishing,
Just about anything you could think of. Also, we did
a lot of traveling
From road trips to plane tickets, every year we try to
make a trip to Mexico.
Still do to this day. Just River, my mom, and me,
going to exotic places.
When we were in-town staying at our mom's for the
most part.
Max and I had chosen to take 6th grade at
Lewis and Clark,
Carpooling every morning and cutting it close
Almost every day with time. Then right after
School going to either Max's or my house,
Usually going and playing football or whatever
we could think of.

The Doctrine of Signatures

Melissa Kwasny

> *Given my disposition, I will always be*
> *circuitous, precocious, an Embellisher.*
> —Lucie Brock-Broido

Given my character, I will always be
the fir out my window—slow to act, to
make decisions.

Given my disposition, I will live my life in one place,
not trembling like the aspen, but swaying
like the heavy spruce, troubled by forces larger than
me—

the moon, the stars, the sun. Do you know
what *radiant*
means, I asked the pretty child at the party
who was not aware of the word that
she was wearing.

When you come—the beginning of a letter
I wish to write,
when you come, this summer, when you stay
with me.

Given my disposition, I will always be retractable,
with my father's long hands and feet.
If I want, glittered and posturing. If I don't, like
the willow,

slouching. Given my temperament, I can be found
where the wood-orchid spreads, under an
awning of rings.
In the pale hour, before dawn, which belongs
to deer—

lithe, running, quiet, observant. Form is often
of the essence.
Given my disposition, in old age, I will be sober
as wind.

MARIANNE BRADLEY
Billings Career Center

9th Grade English Period 1

My Name

Dashiel Brubaker

Were my name a color it would be yellow
For I may be compared to the color for
    its basic-ness

If my name were a day it would be a sunny fellow
Like a sunny day I am liked by others

Were my name a car it would remind you of a
    compact bee
For I am gentle, yet defensive when necessary

If my name were a plant it would be a pine tree
Like a pine tree I survive the harsh Montana winter

Were my name an animal it would be a panda bear
For I may be strong, but at times a bit lazy

If my name were a feeling it would be one of care
Like one who cares I look after others

Were my name a sight it would be snow
For like a snowflake I enjoy traveling in open air

I like my name, I hope you know
Now I must go

Music

Blake Cowen

Music is the ocean
Its currents always making me mesmerized
Music is the lightning
Always leaving me electrified
Music is my medicine
When I'm feeling blue
Music is my best friend
Always helping me pull through
Music is always there
No matter how I'm feeling
When others don't seem to care
Music is like a syndrome
A contagious feeling you can catch anytime
Music is my home
A place where I feel I belong
Music

The Beginning

Maiya Easton

Everyone has a story to their beginning.
Some of us were born prematurely,
Others of us were born large and chubby.
But my story is different than that.
My story began as a secret,
As many of the children of my birth country are.
Our mothers hid their bellies for nine months
In fear of what the government might do.
In a country that's overflowing with people
ripping at the seams with too many babies.
In a country with a rich history and culture
But who can't feed all of its citizens.
In a country that has laws in place to limit the amount
    of children with traditions honored for centuries.
I am a girl. Are you surprised? Most of the babies
    abandoned are girls.
Because boys are more valuable to a family,
Because boys are deemed more valuable on
    planet Earth.
My mother kept me for one day
Before leaving me at an orphanage,
An overcrowded orphanage.
But I'm one of the lucky ones.

When I was 18 months I was adopted into the
  United States
By an American family.
My past circumstances make me who I am.
They give me a sense of pride. They make me
  different: special.
Today, I am an American
Among many other Americans
With a unique beginning.

Family

Ethan Goldhahn

My family is always working.
My mother and father are always wanting the best,
Always telling me to get a job.
My mom doesn't like hers,
Neither does my dad,
Yet they continue to work.
I have applied for many and more to come.
My brother is younger,
But is always striving for the basketball team.
We all look forward to the weekend.

Lost

Isaiah Harris

I lost a friend today
I said some words no one should say
I watched her face change
And then I watched her walk away

Poem of Lies

Liam Mays

This is but a poem of lies
Somehow still filled to the brim with truth
Only I wouldn't let this be seen

I am not what I appear to be
If I had only stayed true
I went on the adventure of life
Never truly caring why

There is nothing I bear
No wounds to repair
And five years of losing ground
To a real me if I had stayed in line

The mirror that I once looked upon
That showed me bright and true
Now shows a cloak that represses the true mind
And makes me a person undefined

A mountain of time I climb
Looking towards the peak
I look towards myself who's making friends
    at the top
And I stand below mesmerized

All my energy is spent
I must find myself and repent
And realize that my own demise
Can come from a poem of lies

I Am

Tristan Peter

Am I strong?
No, I am intelligent.
Am I a painter?
No, I am an artist.
Am I sensitive?
No, I am empathetic.
Am I a writer?
No, I am a reader.
Am I strange?
No, I am unique.
Am I a lover?
No, I am a friend.
Am I fast?
No, I take my time.
Am I a warrior?
No, I am a defender.
Am I focused?
No, I was born to wander.
Am I perfect?
No, I am me.

Winds

Wyatt Peters

I was born in Athens, Georgia.
The winds are quiet, stagnant, calm,
Only stirring on a few
Rare occasions.
We moved to Cora, Wyoming—
My sister introduced
To the world that we all knew;
She's just a baby.
We moved to Pinedale, Wyoming,
Peaceful, far away.
I'd spend my days out in the woods
In quiet solitude.
We moved to Laramie, Wyoming,
To ugly, city life.
Life was somewhat boring,
Laramie, I didn't like.
We moved to Serenbe, Georgia,
The last of the quiet winds,
Playing outside all the time,
Spending time with my friends.
We moved to Tyrone, Georgia,
That's where the winds began.
My new brother came into my life
Shifting my time I had.

We moved to Peachtree City,
One of my favorite spots.
Yet at the same time
The wind blowing like a whirlwind.
We moved to Molt, Montana,
A whole new place
Far away from what I know.
The winds calm, for now.

My Name?

Brennen Wilson

What is my name?
My name is nothing special.
My name doesn't make me me.
It's a pretty uncommon name.
It's not very unique, I was named after someone.
It's a nice name, I'm not complaining,
But there's so much more to me than my name.
Without my name you'd still know who I was.
My name does not define me.
Your name does not define you.

WANDA MORALES
Billings Career Center

9th Grade Honors English Period 3

I Have Boundaries

Riley Anderson

I have social boundaries
I have mental boundaries
I have emotional boundaries
I have physical boundaries
I have family boundaries

A Letter for My Mother

Crucito Aquilar

my mother
a pact, I bequeath to you
to be there when you need me
to love you when you need it the most
a hero through the jungle
protecting you from the most danger
for you are a woman I love
you've held my hand
you've watched me play
you've wiped away my tears
you've helped me get over my fears
but where would I be without you? lost
in a fog
in life
you are the one,
my mother, *my family*

Searching for Glory

Kaedence Eames

I feel inner peace is achieved from a state of bliss,
      but reaching this place is foreign land.
It's land with rolling hills of ups and down, and with
      clouds so defined they appear fake.
This land is full of uncertainty, explaining why it's
      been avoided for so long.
But underneath the grass and trees lies an adventure
      to find the routes of your peace.
I found my peace with music, with the thought of new
      experiences, and with the little moments.
I found my peace within the rays of sunshine
      that seep through my window, and inside
Rain droplets that splash against the ground.
This land explained the sublimity of life, and taught me
      that happiness comes in unconventional
Ways, allowing for both passion and beauty.

Tangible Sadness

Kaedence Eames

Dear Aspen,
When you died, I died too.
My world collapsed. I felt as if I couldn't
   breathe anymore.
It wasn't hard to tell what was going on the morning
Mom received the call. It wasn't hard to
   decipher her
Saddened eyes and choked backed tears.
I wish you could see the way dad cried,
The way mom tried to conceal her sadness,
And the look of pain when we accidentally use
   your name.
I wish you could see the way we felt for you
And understand that I miss you more than anything.

I don't know if you know it, but I've been
   thinking of you
Since you left. I pretend it didn't happen,
   pretend you've
Only gone out for a walk and that you're on your
   way home
Soon. But soon just keeps getting further away.
How long will it be before soon is completely
   out of reach?

How long will it be before all that's left are
    polaroid pictures
And the memory of your face that comes with the
    brisk chilliness
Of a windy spring day?

I remember the way you loved to run, how you
    raced through
The weeds to catch grasshoppers, and barked
    when someone
Sneezed. I miss the way you were scared
    of dad yelling
At the football games, and how you begged
    for ice cubes
From the freezer. You were irreplaceable, and yet I
    look everywhere
To try and fill the hole you left. I was given a sense of
    what it was like
To love unconditionally, and for that, I cannot thank
    you enough.

I Am the Things
I Choose to Be

Abrielle Hillius

I am the things I choose to be
Not what others want me to be
I am the rock against the waves
I am the tree that stands against the wind
I am the sun behind the clouds
I am a dam that holds the water at bay
I am the grass that whistles in the wind
I am crisp cool air of the night sky
I am the stars that shine through the darkness of the night
I am an eagle that sits high in the trees
I am the things I choose to be
Not what others want me to be

Hiking with My Family

Abrielle Hillius

I breath in the crisp, cool air. I feel a peace
Hiking along the spiky mountains.
Near an almost glass-like lake
I hear the fishing pole crack against the wind,
Its sharp whistle against our ears,
The crunch of the rocks beneath our feet
As we walk along the trail,
The trees so high you can't see of what lies beyond.
You place your hand into the cold, blue water,
Wishing you are nowhere else.
Being with my family in this glorious place,
Glad that I have them by my side.

The Beach

Abrielle Hillius

I see my mother lying in the crystal-like sand
The sun rays hitting her skin making it almost glow
Her hair brown like a piece of chocolate
In the distance you can hear the waves crash against
each other
The smile on her face shows that this is her
favorite place
She was so at peace falling asleep on the
fluffy white towel
The salty air water spraying on her face
And in this moment I knew she was happy

Riding, Driving, Nothing

Morghann Kuntz

Driving was one of her many strengths
It was not her first time on the road

Hot July day
The black tar of the road sweats
Excited to celebrate the 4th of July
The smell of the prairie grass on the wind
She never could have expected this to happen
WE never could have expected it to happen
WE never would have expected IT to happen
But then it did
It happened and there is nothing I can do about it
Nothing I can do
Nothing I can do
Nothing I can do
Nothing I could ever do
Nothing that will change the outcome

BOOM!
It is all over
In one instant
done

Spiral

Morghann Kuntz

When you are falling aimlessly to the point of no return
Down the spiral of feelings
When you have lost all control
But you have to put on your face of pure control
What
Went
Wrong
I have no idea who I am or who I want to be
I have no idea what I want to do
I have no idea
What
Went
Wrong
It all is just too much sometimes
I want it to stop
I wanT iT tO stoP
I waNT IT TO stOP
I wANT IT TO sTOP
I WANT IT TO STOP
I want it to stop
What
Went
Wrong
I want it to stop

I need it to stop
I need to shut off my emotions so I can get
    through the day
What
Went
Wrong
I need time
But I can't have time
Time is good
Time is valuable
Time is needed
But time is toxic
Time makes me crazy
Time makes me want things that I can't have
Time makes me wish that I just had one
    more second
To talk to that person
What
Went
Wrong
Sometimes you need time
Sometimes you need time to go away
Sometimes you just need
Need for the things that are lost
Need for the
Need for the spiral to stop

Anxiety

Kira Leone

"Don't worry," they say
As if that will make it better
But on the inside
I'm a wreck
I can't live my life to the fullest
I can't try new things
I can't get past this awfulness inside of me that they
  call anxiety
It's much more than a word, though
It's much more than a feeling
It's a way of living
My whole life revolves around it
It follows me around like a shadow
Doesn't let me do things
It stays with me all day
But I shove it deep down and put on a happy face

Who Am I?

Kira Leone

I don't know exactly who or what I am.
I don't know exactly where I belong
Or who I belong with.
I think that I am still learning about myself everyday
And I can't put myself into words.
I don't know who I am,
But I know that I am much bigger than a poem.
I can't take everything that I am and put it
 into words.
I can't take the feelings,
The thoughts,
The actions,
The love,
Or the hate,
And translate them into words for others
 to understand.
I am more complex than a poem.
But that's the beauty of this amazing life we all live.
We get to learn about ourselves every day.
Maybe when we're older we'll know who we are.
Maybe when we're older we'll know where we fit in in
 this world.
Maybe we will be as lost as we were when we
 were young.

Maybe we will be even more confused
As we have gone through this crazy world.
But maybe we will learn exactly who we are.
Maybe then we can put into words the thoughts
And feelings that we experience.
Maybe then I can put what I am into a poem.
Maybe then I will know who I am.

I Go to the Mirror

Maddelyn Ludwick

I wake up in the morning.
I feel good about myself.
I get up and go to the mirror.
I just see acne on my face.
I get down on myself.
I say, "I am ugly."
I wonder why acne was a thing.
I put makeup on to cover my acne.
I feel good again.
I get to school.
I judge myself again.
I can still see my acne and everyone else can too.
I feel all day that people are judging me because
   of my acne.
She is ugly, no one likes her because she has acne,
   who would be friends with her.
I just want to go home.
I got home.
I just want to be alone, but I also just want
to talk to one person who gets me.
I need someone who can tell me that I am wrong that
   people don't judge me.
I start to feel good and happy on what I look
   like again.

I like my makeup again.
I wished I could be like that all day.
I take off my makeup and see my acne again.
I once again get upset about what I look like
because my makeup is off and I can see
All of my acne again. I feel like it will never
   go away.
I see a bunch of pictures of these beautiful girls
   that do not have acne,
And I want to look like that.
I say over and over again, "I wish I had that."
I go to bed and don't think about myself.

On Being Alone

Maddelyn Ludwick

I can see myself
Walking on the dock
As the beautiful orange and yellow sunrise emerges,
Wishing there were someone to enjoy the
   sunrise with me.
But there is not, so I feel alone.
I just want to go home, but I will be alone at
   home too.
I want to stay in my favorite place
Because of its beautiful views, and it's so quiet.
I like to be alone sometimes but not all week.

Every Morning

Maddelyn Ludwick

Every morning I try to get up
to run down the roads to hear the birds
To smell the dew on the trees
I want to get up
I need something to make me get up and run
But now I have a puppy
Will she want to run with me
Will she be the one there for me

City on the Rise

Nathan Nguyen

A city that is accelerating with modern buildings.
  Respectful people who are always considerate
  and helping others;
    Diverse people who carried their stories like
    stones before they called it home,
    Who can now tell those stories in groups or
    around the fire.
A place that excels in sports, the fans roar and
scream after each touchdown.
  A Montana stadium in blue and gold
    Sandwiched between Missoula and Billings.
Mountains, from the Tobacco Roots to the Crazies,
surround a city full of life and opportunities.
One mountain contains the Big M, whose views from
the Big M will always take the breath out of you.
A place where multiple family members go for an
education.
A place that focuses heavily on engineering
and education.
                    The place is Bozeman.

When I Look in the Mirror

by Faith Smith

When I look in the mirror
I see a girl whose mind controls her.
It imprisons her in a way she can't escape.
When I look in the mirror
I see a girl with pretty blue eyes
With a torment whirling behind them:
A river of thoughts
All branching off,
A tree of emotion and thought and whispers.
When I look in the mirror
It's as if I'm watching through a first-person screen;
I'm not actually there.
My mind is more active
And my world is mere imagination.
My memory is faded.
The moment something passes,
It's out of mind,
Forgotten.
Perhaps it was my imagination.
Perhaps it never happened.
It makes no difference.
When I look in the mirror
I see a girl who lacks feelings.
Her touch is numb

And her eyes won't take in her surroundings to
   their fullest.
She's forever lost in the chains of her mind,
And if she tries to escape, she will fail.
Her efforts exhaust her, and her head begins to hurt.
When I look in the mirror,
Sometimes I think, "That's me."
And I really feel it.
Although it doesn't last, I feel it.
When I look in the mirror,
I see hope.
A small knowing I'm human.
A small whisper in the back of my head
Telling me I'm real,
Everything's real.

Worden

by Faith Smith

The old green bar on the corner of the road
Was a sign I was nearing my place
Of butterflies and horses,
Of bread rolls and mints,
Of warm summer nights making s'mores
   and laughing,
Of a field of grasshoppers and long yellow grass,
Of a single two-story house that sits at the end of the
   gravel road.
The mountains sit faded in the background.
A couple sits on the porch waiting for me—
   my grandparents.
A feeling of joy and excitement fills the air
   as I prepare
For the amazing day to come.
Cicadas scream in the distance,
My grandfather's smile radiates love,
And the house fills with the scent of warm
   fresh bread.
I hear a camper pull into the driveway
And hurry down the porch stairs to them.
My other grandparents emerge from the camper,
Smiling and greeting me.
They hand me mints, the only ones I liked.

Worden became my safe place,
I filled it with as many memories as a
   five-year-old could.
When the visits stopped,
I didn't realize for a very long time
That I had lost the best part of my life.
His memory continues to stick with me,
And so does his smile.
That house will always be a part of me
And so will he.

Now She's Gone

Pacey Tedrick

Every day I can see her there, sitting on the hill staring into the sunset. So blissful yet so very sorrowful. Kept everything on the inside leaving only what she wanted to be seen on the outside. And now she's gone. It makes me wonder what was she thinking. What could I have done to help. I wish she would have said something. I wish she would have let somebody know, but she was in pain. Very grueling pain. We miss you, Emma. Rest in peace.

Winter Wasteland

Jaxton Whitaker

It was winter in Montana,
Winds at 70 mph.
Oh, how I love
This winter wasteland.

The snow is level
With your knees.
Oh, how I love
This winter wasteland.

When you take a breath
Your nose will freeze.
Oh, how I love
This winter wasteland.

Yet kids are still
Wearing shorts.
Oh, how I love
This winter wasteland.

WANDA MORALES
Billings Career Center

9th Grade Honors English Period 4

Where I Am From

Miakoda Brien

I am from stories and campfires on breezy
   summer nights.
My family is made of something harder than rock,
   everyone loves everyone.
Some members within it are more distant,
But all those involved with one another love each
   other so much.

My childhood was swollen with moments together
   with my family,
Potlucks and birthdays and holidays spent together
   over dinner.
Camping trips where you fall asleep to the sound of
   lapping water.
People telling you how beautiful you've gotten,
And how much you've grown.

Everyone always has something to share,
Everyone's ears wide open to receive anecdotes
   from others.
The endless tales of aunts' and uncles' and parents'
   childhoods.
We stay up for hours, telling stories one after another,

Some are sad, some have been told a million
   times before,
But all of them hold a special place in everyone's hearts

The love in my family is indescribable.
And that's what makes losing them so much harder.
Grandmas, Grandpas, Aunts, Cousins.
All the people that meant the world to so many
   people, pass.
Rez folks that were like family, missing.
Such a generous amount of love to give.
Less and less people to give it to as the years go by.
And that's what makes every single moment with
   them so precious.
Knowing you may have to live without them makes
   you love them more.

I Am

Miakoda Brien

I am a small, two-bedroom apartment in a strip of
  blue buildings
They creak and splinter as the years go by

I am the dust that stirs in the cul-de-sac, the dust
  that blinds
A small boy riding his bike when the wind picks up

I am the leaf that drifts to the still watercourse below
The ditch in the backyard sounds of splashing
  water and laughter

I am the melty cheese of a casserole in a
  hand-me-down pan
The aroma that fills the rooms makes
  everyone salivate

I am a small primary school with a tiny playground
Children always leave, but the memories they make
  stay forever

I am the mother of the troubled little neighbor
I sit in the recliner as my young daughter traumatizes
  other little kids

I am the regrets and guilt of a small, confused child
Was this supposed to happen? Who knows?

I am the blood that rushes to the face of a girl whose
   crush is nearby
She flutters her eyelashes and flaunts her neglected
   teal jacket

I am the fright of an abandoned little boy
Rain starts to speckle the sidewalk, a loamy smell
   rises into the air

I am the murky lake that a group of friends sneak out
   to swim in
The stars dance in the sky as the group has the time
   of their life

I am the remorse of a mother with one less child
The smell of alcohol permeates the room

I am the clean pages of a little tan book
An adolescent girl leaves the school library with a
   familiar novel

I am family, I have plenty of love to give
And I am the rising moon and the setting sun

Children turn into elders, and stories turn into legend

River

Miakoda Brien

her fingers reaching out
to touch the concave and bulging earth
that surrounds her body
curvy and ever moving
she never stops
no obstacle
no...

what is this?
a manmade cutoff
concrete and cracking
this wall wasn't here before!
her body swells and overflows
kissing the bank's emerald hair
this is no good

but what is that?
a speck
a moving speck
a human speck!
it greets other moving specks
working, talking, happy
the sweet, bouncy sound
specks are laughing

the specks congregate
congregation
the specks work together
to make buildings and parks
communities are made
the river smiles
the dam, not for naught!

The Clouded Waters

Ashya Clay

I cannot express the depth of my emotions
The clouded waters in my mind never seem
  to recede
I wrestle with the rolling waves in my head
Every time I reach the surface, they come
  crashing down
So strong I am overcome
I think now, now I can finally let them escape
But trapped they remain, pulling me back under
Drowning me as I scream, gasping for air
I flail and kick, but to no avail
Drowning yet still breathing, my heart still
  strongly beating
Begging and pleading to be known

Home

Ashya Clay

Slow music driving down the freeway. The motion of
the car putting me to sleep. Then the ocean, swirling
grey and blue, in the crisp morning air. My toes and
fingers sink softly into the warm golden
sand. Sprinting down the hot pavement in the
blistering sun. Sour lemons, oranges, kumquats, lines
of small potted plants, always ripe with flavor,
sprinklers running back and forth for hours in the
plastic green grass. The sweet smell of hibiscus
flowers and saltwater taunting my senses. Abundant
smiles and laughter among the blue hummingbirds
flitting purposefully from flower to flower. I am home,
I am where I belong.

Places

Ashya Clay

I am California saltwater and late nights on the beach.
I am big city lights and blistering Nevada heat.
I am Montana friendships and my first white
    Christmas snow
I am stronger through my struggles, the reasons I left
Finding a new normal can feel like an uphill battle
But the places this life has led me, I could not be
    more grateful

Rustle of Leaves

Tobin Edwards

In the mountains
By a winding shallow creek
I was walking alone pondering the day
Then to my left I heard the rustle of some leaves
I craned my neck to look
I glimpsed a buck about a foot shorter than me
In two leaps he was in front of me and
    hopping over the creek
The way the sun hit him like one
    of the pictures out of a wildlife magazine
He waited a second, eyeing me, then took off
But not too quickly so I tried to follow him
By about the time I got to where I saw him
I heard another rustle and he was behind me
It was almost like he was messing with me
I blinked and then he was gone,
    never to be seen by me again

Nature's Reflections

Tobin Edwards

If I were an animal
I would be a wolf
Relying on my close pack
Stronger together
But also strong alone

If I were a plant
I would be a raspberry bush
Shy and defensive
Until you get to know me
Then I become kind

Rivers of Love

Tobin Edwards

I am from a place of love
I am from a community of family
I am a from a house of happiness
I am from a city of kind faces
I am from the Treasure State
Where the mountains are full of ore
Hills full of deer and elk
Rivers full of trout and ducks
Fields with geese
I am Montana

I Am Not My Name

Evelyn Fanton

I am not my name
But a different version of it
Sometimes I feel above it
But I want to let it go
I'm always winning the wrong games
I am not my name
Because I am a stranger, a nobody to everyone
   I come by
They always think of me as fresh meat
But look at me, I look weak
I am not my name
Because my parents chose my name
And I am not my parents
I am not my name
Because I'm named after someone that's not me
I don't know my name
Because I don't know me
I don't know who I am or who I'm supposed to be
When do I get to know
I have to let go
This person I'm trying to be
She isn't me
But I am not my name
I am several versions of it
Watch me rise above it

Choices

Emily Harmon

Why did you decide for me?
Why should you have the right?
Am I not my own person,
Overflowing with the ability to make my
  own decisions?
And I wonder,
If I'll ever be allowed,
If I'll ever be able,
To choose for myself.
Because now my life is different,
And will never be the same.
I just don't understand,
How you could do this to me.
I guess you just didn't think,
How your choices would affect my life.
Because I will never be able to be
Exactly who I want anymore.

Going Back

Emily Harmon

Do you ever think back
To those warm Colorado days?
My memory is filled with gleaming sunshine
Reflecting off the fresh coat of snow.
Then we walk through miles of it
Just to reach the point
We've been scouting for weeks.
I'm filled with the alluring beauty of the colors
   around me,
So we take off our gloves
And build him
And admire his strange charm;
And then, I feel such immense joy.
I don't know if I'll ever feel the same again.
We pack our stuff back into our bags
And walk all the way back

Our snowman lasted months
Despite the beating heat of the ruthless sun.
We drove past it everyday
Thinking back to when we built him,
Thinking of how much we loved each other
   when we hiked there.
I wish I could go back.

Seasons

Emily Harmon

I am the snow gliding gracefully to the ground,
Signifying the first days of winter.
I am the grass getting buried under the cold blanket
  of white.
I am the children creating snow angels,
Excited for the season to come.
I am their parents looking for the heavy jackets
  and mittens.
I am the days slowly getting shorter,
And I'm the extra blankets people put on their beds,
Keeping them warm from the frigid blizzards that are
  to come.

I am the sun coming out from a long rest,
Melting the drifts built from the storm's past.
I'm the flowers beginning to re-bloom in new beauty.
I am the grass growing greener,
And the days growing long again.

I am the children coming out to play,
And the last day of school,
Exciting, and long-awaited.
I am the plans being made
For children to reunite during the long break.

And finally,
I'm the crisp, golden leaves,
Drifting down, down, down,
Until they reach the ground,
To be stomped on by running children.
I am the chilly wind, returning once again,
And the snow eventually beginning to fall anew.

I am the repetitious cycle of seasons:
Winter, Spring, Summer, and Fall.
I am the long awaited,
And the long dreaded, seasons.
Coming time and time again
I am always reliable,
And yet change with the wind.
I am Winter,
Cold and hectic.
I am Spring,
Blooming and beautiful.
I am Summer,
Playful and cheery.
And yet again,
I am Fall,
Graceful and amusing.

What Stops You?

Stecher Hefty

Who stops you from being yourself? Who tells you you're wrong when you express your opinion? Our society is at a point where not being the norm is disgraced. Our changing environment is changing but things will still be judged in the twenty-first century. People will still feel forced to stay within the judgment of society. No one makes society's boundaries. No one said that we couldn't express ourselves or be who we are. And yet every day we hide behind each other scared to be ourselves.

The Camp in the Valley

Sofia Lintern

I sit on the porch swing, swaying slowly in the
   gentle breeze.
In the breeze, the sound of soft music travels.
The wake-up bell rings, its rhythmic pairs of ding-
   dongs sounding.
It is just after sunrise, and I sit with a coffee in hand.
I observe the soft yellows, blues, and pinks of the sky
   nestled between the mountains protecting
   this valley.
I take in the calm.

The sound of children's voices arises as they wake.
I sit and watch as they scatter about the field,
their laughter filling the air,
in harmony with the music that the breeze carries
   throughout the camp.
I love this place.
The calm of the mornings and evenings,
and the busyness of the days.

Something About Memory

Jon Joseph Malaga

I miss the times when things were easy
The times when school was nothing but breezy
Today things are just getting harder and harder
And even more things are being more of a bother
So much work to get finished
That time is now getting more diminished
Nowadays all people think is important
   are commodities
And not the time they spent with their own families
People keep saying how much they learn something
But they never understood if it meant anything
I only wish for the old times to come back
That the things people say were mostly meaningful.

Family

Jon Joseph Malaga

I enjoy time with my family
Knowing that they will always be beside me
My family teaches things I need to know
Many things they teach me will help me grow
They taught me how to care
They taught me how to share
So that one day when I become older
I will enter the world bolder than I was before

Your Annoyingly Long Fingers

Emily Mowat

Although I despise to be alone for too long
I can't attempt to breathe the same air
of the same person for too long
Because it is intoxicating, nauseating,
and it makes me feel out of place.
I get clingy, I need you, I want you,
you are my everything and I can't live without you.
Then I get scared, I convince myself that you hate me,
You want to kill me, you're bored of me, and you
can't stand another minute of me.
Then I don't turn the tables, I push them down
with force.
I hate you, your voice, your personality,
your character,
your TAP TAP TAP of your annoyingly long fingers,
I hate your smile, and your face.
You make me want to die and come back and
kill you.
But I keep it all burrowed, deep and solidified within

Until I break, not erupt, no not like a deadly
volcano that spews
emotion for miles, but instead I will slowly rot
like a corpse,
killing myself with my own imagination. I will
convince myself
that there is nothing more to do but hate you forever
and ever
Although I despise to be alone for too long, with the
risk of getting lost
in my own thoughts. I can easily accomplish
such heights
around people, specifically people that I love.

Writer's Block

Ella Grace Pellandini

The mental border forms in my mind
Words seizing in my conscience
Coming and going as if dropping in to say hi
"Hello writers block"
Creativity bounces around trying to exit
Shifting left to right, up and down
I can't translate the clutter and heap of my brain onto
  my paper
Staring blankly noticing the blue vertical lines
and the one red horizontal line

I Am the Calm River

Emily Pfeffer

I'm the still water
Flowing against the current
Traveling the world

Delicate

Emily Pfeffer

Lilies, so delicate and soft
Their colors so extravagant
Adding color to a bland picture

Worth more than a penny costs
The smell, so contaminant
Their beauty is a restrictor

Maybe lilies are what I got
Lilies are what I am, and
Their beauty is my structure

FREE VERSE INSTRUCTORS

Nicole Gomez
Taylor White
Silas Miller
Lorna Buckingham
Olivia Round
Sam Dunnington
Nikki Zambon
Landen Beckner
Jesse Nee-Vogelman
Claire Compton
Sam Hines

Never Forget Family

C.T.S.

when i think of my mother i think of what she is
doing, crossing the sky like an eagle watching all the
pain and fear course through my body, watching my
family even though we cannot see her, trying to have
our backs even though she is not here, battling every
war with us even though she is only in my heart.

Pain & Anger

C.T.S.

All i feel is pain and anger all i want to do is just forget what happened but it's just burning me like a torch to skin when i'm alone it hits me drives me crazy and it's just nothing but pain this pain is like rain it just showers me with pain and anger and pain and anger is like a waiter they both serve you in a way sometimes in a good way and in a bad way but sometimes you can feed off of what it is giving you and then you can forget but like some things, it stays there and doesn't leave and stays with you your entire life and then you finally let it go but it just tears you apart but you got to remember if you get up and walk it off it heals and then you feel better and you can go on without pain and anger and then you can tell that waiter to get the check and then walk out with nothing on your mind and then you are smooth as wind then you can let your mind unwind then you and her are free she is free to walk you are free to talk without pain and anger then you can also think without pain and anger and you never have to see that waiter again.
R.I.P MOM

The Battle

C.T.S.

i battle my anger like i'm in a street fight, i tell it to go then it strikes, i battle it to leave me the fuck alone, i battle it so i don't hurt someone that i care for, i battle it so much that i die from not breathing, i am in a constant fight every day with it sometimes i win sometimes i get stomped but no matter what i battle that asshole till he quits and decides to finally fuck off.

What My Days and Nights Look Like

C.T.S.

What my morning days and nights look like is long filled with hell and working out dealing with the same people every day sleeping in a cell that smells like sewers through the vents waking up to someone over an intercom getting pissed because i am still here in the same cell same bed in the same place and can't go anywhere but a damn dayroom that isn't any bigger than this classroom maybe a little bigger but not much and thinking about the same shit every damn day.

Wings

KACP

there's not a day that goes by that i don't think of you
your voice like a lullaby
your eyes like a forest of chestnuts
your skin, tan like summer
i know you never got the chance to be yourself,
and i guess i should've seen it.
all the hurt you were holding back
all the tears you shed
but i know that you're in a better place,
able to be yourself and happy
I know that heaven's given you a second chance.
your wings were ready.

Poem in 152 Days (5 months)

KACP

the 1,064 times i kissed you
the 912 times i said "i love you"
the 608 times i hugged you
the 3 times you saw me cry
the 1 time i said "goodbye"
in the end you were ready, but my heart was not

Walls

KACP

Thought I had eyes like obsidian, too dark to see
  through to my soul.
And a heart made of tungsten, too strong to break.
So congratulations, because my heart is the hardest
  to break and my soul was barely visible.
I told you I don't let people close because I'm afraid to
  get hurt, and that I tend to only push people away.
I tried my hardest and completed these walls I built
  up only to have you destroy them.
You told me you loved me, and I was foolish enough
  to believe you.
'Cause all you did was tear me apart and damage me
  beyond repair.
I learned my lesson.
I built walls higher than Burj Khalifa.
I vowed after you to never let anyone break down my
  walls or even let them down for anyone.
I don't mean this in a malicious way.
I still love and care about you, though I don't
  know why.

I've come to realize that maybe you enjoy hurting
  people because you're afraid you'll get hurt.
That's all right.
But it won't be that way forever.
All you need to do is think about it.

IT-Emotions

Lone Owtkasd

Let's see…
I was 3
On my knees
When God spoke to me
I was a slave
Never free
Like I'm supposed to be
Dad was brown as a tree
Mom was white as could be
Both a nic and crack fene
Never thought I'd make it to 18
Again on my knees and my face went green
When I looked up at momma's face
I could tell she was pleased
Dad found out later
Then he made me bleed
Had to plead
No more belt
He was drunk
Didn't know how he felt
Later I found out
It was the drugs he dealt
On his breath the smoke I smelled
A place in my heart he held

Never tell
That's my gangster life hell

[PAUSE]

I was 4
Never lookin' more poor
Went to the store
While daddy wasn't lookin'
Mommy sold 'erself like a whore
Down with the door
I was on the street that mornin' little past 4
It opened my core
'Fore I left
Took the pistol out my junk drawer
Saved me from getting mugged
What better could I ask for?

[Shorter PAUSE]

I was 5
Feds cookin' dad like a chive
Aye
Then he got sported
My life all distorted
The coke my momma snorted
Too high
Can't 'member where she stored It
Had to leave town
Trynna floor It
Feds on our ass

Trynna run
Couldn't afford It
My gangster like shorted
While this song bein' recorded
"The fuck was I thinkin'?" I retorted
Child
Spouse abuse and
Bye
Bye dad
He was long gone deported
Sat out on the porch wit my toy box while
    it was pourin'
Waitin' for my new life
Man
Waitin' is so borin'
Think my pain hurt so bad nobody was scorin'
Couldn't tell if I needed a drag or Neosporin
Finally
Was at grannies
Shit was so foreign
I didn't realize that this was just a lure in
Momma said goodbye 'fore I recognized the floorin'
Aye
Baby sister was just born
Thought I was forsworn
But before I could do anything
It was off with the clothes I worn
Too dirty
Too torn

'Bout 11:30 and it was still pourin'
Took a bath and I felt important
Cuz back on the streets
We wasn't washin'
We was endurin'
That's the curtain
But not really
They thought I was just silly
I was actually feelin' a killy
Anger levels goin' over a trilly
Then grandpa started actin' like a goddamn hillbilly
Left our family so far behind
Like he went to philly
Hit me 'bout a trilly
I always said, "not really"
Granny bust out the broom
Hit me in my room
Teachers
Friends
Trynna assume
It just made 'er fume
I knew if I didn't shut up, I was at my doom
Then came the big boom

[PAUSE]

Pictures Ugly
The big 1-0
The divorce
I just said whom was whom

It came
It went
It killed 'er heart
It took 'er sweedom
Woulda' left me in a tomb
But I had Spider-Man
There so soon
It was crazy
Like a hobbit
No way to stop it
Moved from my best friend
Started with the border hoppin'
Face croppin'
In all those yearbooks

[PAUSE]

Turnin' 13 was all it took
Think how spooky it looks
With only 1 hispanic in your picture books
It took my life
It took my freedom
Always gettin' beat up
Tossed 'round every which way
I met a girl and stayed
But all she did is play
Played me for my best friend
I was at the end
Started smokin' and drinkin'
It was my new trend

Never again get offend
In fact, started to defend
Fam saw me bend
Turned 14 and away I was sent
Out to boys' homes and hospitals
Always got kicked out
Floppin' like some trout
Cryin' like a waterspout

[PAUSE]

15 and I'm lookin' stout
Figured this was what life was 'bout
Met a redneck girl
She was tricky like a Tech Deck
Wasn't no easy picnic
Love gets me so sick
Already on probation
But lovin' the sensation
Don't care 'bout our destination
All we needed was a reservation
But didn't have no preparation
Not long often
I was long gone again
Came back and committed worst sin
I tried to die
And be born again
She was gone with a different man
Tried to hide the pain
But it poured down my brain

Left a bloody stain
Left me in disdain
Tried to be a rapper
But
No gain
With no fame
Tried to keep tame
But was gone with the wind and the rain
Life hit me like a train

[PAUSE]

Was 16 goin' through it all again
Gone for 10 months and fell in love
Fast again
We made love and were stuck
Surprised at my luck
Shoulda' took the hit
Never try to duck
Bloody on the floor
The resolution
To my marriage no more
Went away
Came back
With a plan of attack
Got a tack cut my wrists
Couldn't deal with the bliss
Didn't deserve
Quite a curb
Never feel superb

Got in fights
But stayed sober
Then I was deterred
Brother S was dead
I washed over like a blur
Started drinking
Trynna die
It was what I earned
Got some treatment
Knockin' on death's door
Moppin' up death's floor
Workin' my life wit every chore
Skin got tore
Beatin' out of bore
To a bloody pulp
That just like a cult
It was blue
You know who
Joined up red
Just to let my life go ahead
Almost dead
Now a rapper
Trynna make some bread
Hidin' from the feds
Keep my life on speed

[PAUSE]

Now 'bout 17 wit no dreams
Surprised I made it this far

Now gotta die hard
Now in jail
This is what I've learned
Don't take life for granted
If you do
You'll have marks
From the pain
From the guilt
From It
The never-ending burn

Response to Philadelphia Street Art

MEC

The shapes are really cool in their droopy ways. The purple blue shape has a golden tooth and is right next to red which is a cyclops. Most of the shapes get gradually bigger as they go down the line.

Cheating

R

the swaying movement in eyes that indicated lying
the smell of old liquor on her breath
the obvious dark purple suck marks below her chin
the denying on top of denying with a touch of
  hard truth
the wanting to leave and never coming back
  came eventually

To Prisoners

RHC

I call for you to stay in the right state of mind
To see what is right not wrong
Learn from mistakes that have led to
Be the best person humanly possible
To *never* come back

Response to the Ptolemaic View of the Universe by Andreas Cellarius

RHC

Am baby
Holding my mf ball
This lump of flesh is angry
I have thy ball twas not his
He shall receive once mwah is done
In meantime I'm just chillin

List of Five Things I Know to Be True

RHC

1. Birds aren't real
2. Coconuts are mammals
3. "Apple" is pronounced "Bapple"
4. I miss my ex
5. Money isn't the root of evil, people are

Unnamed Drawing of a Girl

RK

My girlfriend drew me a picture in pencil and she said underneath "this is just some random girl," but it looks a lot like her although it is not her. The picture comes alive at night and she winks and moves her lips as if she wants a kiss. She makes me feel as if she is with me and not so far away.

When i'm lonely i look at the picture and i think about her and all the memories that we have made and i wonder if i will live long enough to make a thousand more and millions after. When I look at the picture I think that i want to make a life with her and possibly have children too but with this virus killing everybody i don't even know if i will live long enough to fulfill my future as a man who made a 360 with his life and became the great loving caring father that he never had and made life worth living like his father never did. When i look at the picture of her it's like i'm looking into the future with a telescope or really far down a dark dark tunnel and seeing the light that was never there.

It's funny how someone can make you feel as if the world is great and nobody is doing drive-bys or killing, kidnapping innocent people. It's like she makes me think as if the world is perfect and no harm can be done to anyone, as if she were a drug that i use to take me to another level to deal with anxiety and depression and escape the pain this world has to offer but lead me to a reality that no one else can see but me.

Everyone thinks that people always use drugs to escape reality, but I use them to bring me to it. I'm going to prison and that picture of the girl she drew helps me escape the fact that i've made 24 major mistakes and makes me look at how i can make millions of achievements and grow as a human being and as a man and help people who are like me and never had anybody to help them through their struggles. I can be the person to light their candle in their dark room. I can possibly lead them down the road that never ends, one that has many beautiful sights to see, one that you don't have to pay to get there.

Many people I know struggle with addiction and loneliness but just because they use drugs doesn't make them a bad person. Some of the most loving and caring people are addicted to some kind of drug. Most just use to numb their own pain so they can feel others' pain and help them. when people say you can't help people unless you help yourself first is not true... It's not, i've seen so many addicts help even sober people. People don't just use it because they know it's bad, they use to shut up the voices in their head screaming at them that they're not good enough and the screaming voice in their head called sadness telling them to kill themselves. I, RK, have witnessed firsthand that drugs can save lives but they also can take them just as quickly.

Every time i have a craving i think of my 2-year-old niece and the woman who drew me that picture and i realize that no matter how bad it gets i will never have to use again and ruin the joy that those two will give me "ever." When I stare at the picture of the girl in the dim light and it winks at me it's almost as if it's E. winking at me telling me it will be ok, i'm here with you. And suddenly a weight has been lifted from my shoulders and i can breathe again, i can focus. I know that when i get out she'll be there waiting for me and we can start our lives and with her love i can stay sober, and with me sober she can feel my love and know that it's real that it's deep that it's true. Our relationship isn't perfect but whose is? I'm not gonna lie, she runs away quick when things get bad but runs back just as fast if not faster when i better myself, man up, admit that it was my fault she left and just say sorry.

But it's not about saying sorry it's about meaning it when you say it and proving it to the person you're saying it to and showing them you mean it, saying sorry is a promise that you didn't mean to do or say what you did that made you say sorry in the first place. It's also a promise that you will go to any extent to better yourself and never do it again to the best of your ability. Saying sorry is about showing the person you hurt that you feel bad and that it not only hurt them but you hurt yourself too, and you want to move forward in your relationship and make sure the past is the past so you can both move on to better things. When you say sorry… Don't follow it with an excuse or reason either just simply say you're truly sorry. you don't have to explain yourself unless they hit you with the almighty "why." Be a good person and change the world by saying you're sorry and proving you truly mean it.

List of Five Things I Know to Be True

RK

A list of things i know to be true is people that have authority will try to get you to give them information and make you think they will help you but that's all bullshit they try to manipulate you into believing their lies and make you think they will protect you but they won't they get what they want and forget about you I've seen it happen to other people. I hate snitches with a passion and they tried to get me to snitch and i told them to fuck off that it would help them and buy my own bullet like f'real i know how the shit works I've been in the game my whole life and living in Arkansas especially in Little Rock you learn that no one gives a fuck about you and they will do what is beneficial to them at the end of the day. People always wanna be there, ride or die but when they get threatened with jail time they crack easier than an egg, I'm not like that I'm taking a hit and going to prison for some shit i didn't even do. Why? Because I'm loyal and i, RK, know what it's like to be snitched on.

Being a W.

SW

Being a W. is a rough life. Got a family member in jail every other night. Dad just relapsed being an addict is a tough fight, losing family members is the hardest thing in life. We're in such a bad position that we steal from a woman's purse, workin hard to break hold from the devil's curse. I pray to God and ask to make it all better, but sometimes it feels like I'm writing Santa a letter. Oh God please answer my prayers it feels like I'm just talkin lookin at air. Why does life have to be so unfair, yeah half of our cousins are in foster care, life's rough, constantly wanna rip out my hair. Starting to not even care. But our family deserves to live up there. We deserve a nice house with a really nice wife, but being a W. is a rough life, yeah it a rough life. Yeah none of our family go past a 10th grade degree, we all dropped out and went straight to methamphetamine. Yeah momma went broke and had to start pawning things. And as last resort I had started to sling. My childhood was taken way too early, I should still be out chillin on them swings. But when you come from a broken family, you learn to enjoy the little fuckin things. So from then on out I only cared for my mom, but it didn't take long and she was gone. Man why does

God… fuckin hate me, I mean I'm glad she is done with pain and suffering. I am still mad that you took her from me, but I am relieved that she is up there and happy. I just wish I could have one more kiss, now I'm sitting here wanting to slit my wrist. Man why do I have to put up with this, on the inside I'm still just a little kid. Fuck I wish I could just see her smile… But let's pray that it'll be a while. Yeah. Yeah being a W. is a rough life, got a family member in jail every other night. Dad just relapsed being an addict is a tough fight. Losing family members is the hardest thing in life. But all we can do is pray it'll get better as we get older, hold our heads high and keep that shit on our shoulders. Be optimistic hope it all gets bright and nice… but we know being a W. is a rough life!

Beautiful

T

beautiful is a great word it means you are
pretty and no one can take that from you no
matter what you are beautiful in your own
ways don't let anyone tell you otherwise
because they're wrong and you are beautiful
no matter what. don't forget

Poem of an Animal's Life

T

the dog is eating
the cat is hunting
the hamster is running
the fish is swimming
the lizard running

A Prayer in Uncertainty

T

I dont know about these days they're so
  hard it's hard to know right from wrong
I dont know if i can make it to the next day
  because all the bad
Things going on in my life what if i just
  didn't wake up who knows
It's going to be so hard but i know i can
  make it   but there's one
Thing i don't know if i'll see my family ever
  again   it's gonna be
Hard let's pray that i can make it dont know
  if it's gonna happen
But let's pray lord please help me and my
  family come back
To our old lives because i'm here and they're
  home well   i'm
In jail   but just know i'm a believer so i'm
  going to end this song
By saying   amen

CLAIRE MIKESON
Billings Career Center

9th Grade English Period 4

Only Necessities

Carlos Aguirre

When I go backpacking
I bring only necessities
For I know unneeded supplies are
Just extra weight on my back.
Similar to life,
I don't carry stress or worries in my bag,
I bring love and compassion and
Everything I will need on my journey.
Only then, will I have the strength to live my life.

A Fish Story

Jacob Anderson

I smelled the moist dense air
Felt the rock of the waves under my feet
I cast out my line into the raging river
Watched as it bobbed through the current
And it weaves around the white water
Keeping a watchful eye
As I waited in anticipation
I saw a breach
A wonderful glimmering rainbow
Struck the fly dead on
And heaved itself into the air
Like a great white in the Atlantic
So I started to reel as hard a possible
As the trout pulled with the weight of a truck
And as it cut through the water
And up to the rocky riverbank
I pulled it up to the surface
And I saw
In all its magnificence
A miniature brown trout
And a waisted fly in its mouth

This Chalk

Amaya Becker

I enclosed myself with chalk again.
A crooked circle that entraps me and the
  encompassing terrain,
A color that is asleep and unwelcoming.
A color that is chilly, cold,
A color that makes my teeth chatter and
  my skin bump up.

The color,
Like a cloudy, overcast,
Somber day.
Like a gloomy, sick
Ageless week.

Like a dead, pale,
Heavy year.

And the warmth is absent.
There is no sun,
On my chalk-made planet.
It hides behind those nasty clouds,
That never rain.

The chalk misleads me.
It tells me not to leave.
It tells me I was not meant to explore outside
  these lines.

It tells me I am not good enough.
I belong only here, where I am all-knowing
   of the territory,
And I begin to lie to myself too.

I am comfortable here.

I do not mean to scrape the earth around me with it,
I don't know if it is even me pressing this dusty block
To the ground and tracing these lines of
Limitation all around me.
My limitations.
They point their words at me,
My peers 'negative opinions and judgment to me,
The worries and possibility of being put down
   by those I look up to and model.
The fear,
That if I leave, I'll realize the chalk and its lines were
   correct.
And no one will want me.
I cannot seem to erase the lines.
Could you tell me,
Why?

And when I rub my hand to it,
No residue lies on my palm.
And the line does not falter in its pigment.
When I tear at the ground and rake the earth,
The line does not budge.
And people walk past, distant to my problem.
No one will speak to me,

They too are scraping at their own chalk-ridden circle.
With no sun, and no light.
We all sit,
And wait.

Like a Fish

Amaya Becker

Like a fish,
I sit in a bowl.
A bowl full of cold and dirty water,
That holds darkness and silence.

When I bring power to my voice,
I am hushed
By a brittle input.
Could someone be here with me, maybe?
They sound so familiar, too.
Telling me not to say a word, to stay silent
And poised,
To stay perfect.

"You don't want to embarrass yourself,
Do you?"

"No one wants to listen to you."
And yet, I've got no idea who I am to be silent for.
Who do I sit still and calmly for?
Who do I sit in perfection for?
There is no one here.
Only me.
And the voice.

When I try to leave this glass bowl,
I am pulled back in.

And the spoken thoughts tell me to stay:

"You don't want to get lost, do you?"

But there is absolutely nowhere to go.
How can one get lost in a mindless bowl?

Like a fish,
I sit here,
In a bowl that I feel like I am suffocating in.
I am suffocating because I know I am telling myself
    these things.
This voice belongs to no one
But me.
I know I am keeping myself from leaving this dim,
    damp, numbing bowl.
I do not want to be a fish stuck somewhere with small
    surface area anymore, with a very light
Amount of choices and places to explore.
I want to be in the ocean with the other fish, and
    enjoy my time, not a worry that I'll get lost
Or be eaten up by bigger fish.
I want to brush through coral and explore deep into
    the sea's trenches.
I want to get caught in the plants held in the sand as I
    am chased by predators.
I want fear, and excitement, adventure, challenge.
I want it all,
I want all that is not in this bowl.

But it's my fault.
This fishbowl is made of my worries and my fears.
It's written all over.
And it reminds me every day, why I am told not to
     speak or move, leave or do something *different*.
It reminds me that it is my fault
This bowl exists.

Families Need Fathers

Amaya Becker

My father resides only in memory now.
I can barely recall his face, though
I can still see eyes, squinted, tired,
But full of understanding and awareness.
His teeth, once so straight, but now slowly
Rotting away,
Like our relationship.

He wears baggy pants and big boots.
And when I was very little, I'd stick my small feet
Into those big boots and walk around in them.
And I'd think how exciting it'll be when I'm bigger
And older.
And all the things he will teach me,
All the boys he'll shoo away,
All the school dances he'll see me get ready for,
All the music we'll share together,
All the food we'll cook together,
All the nature he'll explore,
All the memories we'll make,
Together.
And it won't hurt
when I think of them.

And his laugh,
It makes me feel so cherished,

So accepted and praised.
And then my request for his love
Is rejected all over again.

And those mountains we climbed when we were
  both younger,
The slipping and the catching of each other,
Like the slipping of his appearance in my mind,
But the catching of it so I don't forget,
So he won't forget.
So he won't forget,
About me.
I remember him.
So he has to remember me,
Right?
Like the slipping of his guidance in my life,
Of his effort in my existence,
The slipping of his worth in my world.
But he never catches himself like I catch me.
He won't catch his responsibilities:
Like being a father to me,
Like showing me that he really cares.

But I think of them.
Those memories.
Those memories that keep grasping at my feet,
Tearing at my jeans, ripping and tugging, wishing to
  be seen,
Wishing to be remembered.

Like a marathon, those memories race from my eyes
   to my chin, and drip to the finish line.
Warm and salted, as they run down my lips.
Painful and unwanted; they sting.
They beg me to remember.
And I don't want to remember.
But if I called,
I hope you'd answer, Dad.

Insecurity

Breana Boehm

My insecurity has gone too far.

I run to the bathroom every time I can,

Talking down to myself, thinking down to myself:

"You're ugly, you're too annoying, you're too quiet,

No courage, your hair is gross, no one will like you,

You're not good enough."

I try not to think about this, but it's a habit.

I don't think I'm gone,

I think, I'm gone.

My life is a mirror, reflecting, making me believe the things I see,

But they're not.

I see what I don't want to,

I see what I think,

But I don't see what I am.

I see the things that are not what I want,

I see the things I don't like.

Why am I like this?

I'm like this cause I'm broken,

I'm like this because I'm hurt,

I'm hurt from what has happened in the past month,
No, year.
I will learn to get better,
I will learn to be better,
I will learn to love myself.

Grass

Elijah Bryan

If I were grass, I would be everywhere.
I could see the smile on people's faces.
I could see the heartbreak couples go through,
Every fight, every make-up, every hangover.
I could see every bride and every groom about to
   get married.
I could see every day until earth is no more,
Every race, color and ethnicity in a person.
I could see civilization grow and grow.
I could hear every word ever made.
I could see every brand of shoe,
Every man, every woman, every dog and cat.
I could speak any language.
I could hear every sound.
I could smell every scent.
I hope to never go extinct.
I will learn new languages.
I will move to other planets.
I will explore new species and cultures and beliefs.
If I were grass, I would be everywhere.

Family Poetry

Lexi Carey

We were a family in the dark
We were new to town
Yet people talked to us
I didn't understand why
We were just ordinary people
But acted like we were special
Our home smelled like pumpkin spice
Those candles were my favorite
They always made me happy
One day I came home and there were people
People I didn't recognize
They kinda looked like my grandparents
But I couldn't tell if it was them or not
Then they said my name and it was different
I never heard that name before
Then someone touched me
And I realized it was a dream
But after that I was so happy
Because of how much I needed my family
to get through life
They helped me even when I did not know
the answer
They made me feel special even when I was *ordinary*
My family is crazy but I still love them

My favorite memory was when my brothers were here
And we played football in the backyard
And even though I did not know how to play
They still accepted me
We laughed when we fell down
And cried when we had to go back inside
But now I still think about them
Even when they are not here
I miss them when they are in Texas
My mom and I look a lot alike
We act like we are related
Even when I don't see her for a while
We had the same hair color till she died it
My grandma and I are so close
She kinda fills the position of a mother to me
My grandpa kinda fills the position of a dad to me
I haven't seen my dad in 11 years but I am still me
And I would change nothing about my family
Not even my slimy hairy pets that I love so much

Memories

Lexi Carey

Memories are special
They are different for everyone
They are either good or bad
For some they are dark
And for some they are bright
They move people everyday
People make choices off of their memories
Memories are unforgettable
They can be dangerous
They help us remember loved ones
That have moved on
I can remember the time we first got a puppy
It was the most exciting time in my life
Memories are a thousand words
You can't quite explain them
They leave you speechless
And confused
I wish I could forget the bad ones
And bring to life the good ones
I wish the good memories popped up
Like the smell of fresh air
Memories are beautiful
They help you remember the ones
That are no longer with us

Or around us
They help you remember
The sweet smell of the flowers
When spring finally arrives
Memories are special

Mystery

Lexi Carey

She was a mystery in the dark
She was as quiet as a mouse
She was afraid of failure
When she looked in the mirror
She saw a stranger looking at her
She was an athlete
She was very complicated
People didn't understand her
They called her names without meeting her
She was competitive with sports
People thought she was a shadow in the dark
She was a busy girl
She had swimming and school
She wanted to be a follower
Instead she stood out
And she was a leader in the community
She didn't recognize herself
She felt alone even when she wasn't
She had friends but some left
She lived with her grandparents
She had animals who loved her
She liked being alone
That meant she had peace in the air
She hated when people talked about her

She thought that they judged her every minute
Her home smelled like pumpkin spice
That made her feel like she was safe
When she walked in she was happy
Even when she was sad
It made her feel free
Not like she was being held in prison
She was a mystery in the dark

In My Home

Keyli Harper

In my home
You will find teenage children,
Our chaotic lifestyle,
But also comfort.

In my home
There are toys everywhere.
There is a foster toddler
Who we care endlessly for.
The sound of that child's laughter fills the house.

In my home
I have a brother.
A brother who's 18 months younger than me.
A brother who's addicted to candy and Coca-Cola.
A brother who keeps my secrets,
But who's also my best friend.

In my home
I have a strong mom.
A mom that goes to bed early.
A mom who has long conversations on the phone
   with her boss,
But also a beautiful woman who has worked harder
   than any woman I know
Just to get where she is today.

In my home
I have a loving dad
Who learned how to love children that weren't his own.
A dad who grew patience,
Who showed us the love we yearned for from
    our father.

In my home
We eat cereal or leftovers when life gets hard.
But when we eat home cooked meals,
Loud music fills our ears from the kitchen.

In my home
My parents double as college students.
They work hard,
But never fail to provide us with what we need:
Like food in our stomachs.
A roof over our heads,
And clothes on our backs.

In my home
Sometimes we fight,
Sometimes we don't get along,
Sometimes we yell things we don't mean,
And sometimes it gets ugly.
In my home
We learn to forgive.
We learn to love and move on.

In my home
We're surrounded with family

And surrounded with love.
Unconditional love.
And joy,
Endless joy.

The Girl

Skarlett Hultman

Having to raise two girls is hard
No mom
No future learning experiences
The girl learned on her own
So she could then teach her sister
The one she raised through the dark times
Their mom a raging alcoholic
Took it out on her own kids
Glass, broken
Skin, bleeding
The pain in her oldest eyes
Could see the pain in her mood-changing eyes
Their mom lied time and time again
Her kids' thoughts were filled with negativity and lies
Her mom made them cry
Her oldest thought she should die
But in the end she made it out alive

Do Not Tread

Ayden Ingraham

Moving along the ground,
Quickly, smoothly, and quietly
Testing the air with its tongue,
Searching and hiding,
But when tested it coils
Up giving warning
With a quiet zzzzzzzz–
And without warning a flash of pink.
When you look down you'll see red
Emphasizing the saying do not tread on me.
For I will hurt you if you try to tread on me.
For I will leave you alone if you do so to me.

My Mirror

Quinn Isakson

When I look into a mirror
I see a smart,
Energetic, young
And wholesome freshman.

I am an athlete,
A strong leader,
A soccer star,
And a loyal friend.

As I look deeper,
I can no longer recognize
This human looking back.
All I see is dark
And small flashes of light.

When the mirror is broken
I see a dark, defeated,
Sad being,
Unrecognized and cracked,
Staring into the abyss.

When the mirror is fixed,
I see a new,
Bright, intelligent mind
Full of energy, life and happiness,

Looking ahead to the future.

These are the features
My mirror shows me.

Family Vacations

Brooklynn Jamieson

Family vacations filled with adventure
Popped tire
I see a bear!
BEES!!!
Snacks at gas stations
Barbeque chips
Gum
Slurpees!
7 packed in the car
Legs piled on top of one another
Game over if someone farts
Crowded
Books on tape with soothing voices telling
   endless stories
The Boy in the Striped Pajamas
Room
Anne Frank's Diary
Car filled with sleeping kids
Mom in front
Taelar, Brook, And Torie in middle
Kadee and Jesse in back
My families vacations
Oregon
Nebraska
Florida

Memories
Too many to count

I Am Me

Brooklynn Jamieson

I am Brooklynn
I am a sister
A daughter
A niece
Me
Ugly
Female
Teenager
I like people
I am an athlete
I can skate
Talkative
Anxious
Loyal
Me
Loud
Different
Crackhead
Photographer
Social butterfly
Complicated
Talented
Unique
Bold
Me
Hurt
Strong
Clumsy
Confused
Reckless

I am insecure
I am always hot
I like social media
I like my phone
Unapologetic
I drink water
Dreamer
Crazy
Cool
Me
Proud
Chubby
I'm vibing
Vanilla smell
I like rap music
I love my friends
And big family
I'm annoyed
Interesting
Emotion
Myself
Sad
Me
Real
Writer
Irrelevant
Classmate
I like stickers
I can be brave
I live in Montana

Geyser

Brooklynn Jamieson

Inside me is a geyser
Waiting to blow a fuse
Over-dramatic and loud
Expected to be unexpected

Why I Am the One Who Listens

Austin Lee

Why do I listen to my peers?
I never get my time,
They never want to hear from me
After I have given them mine.

I only want to be friendly
With all my peers,
But when I see them
They act like I haven't seen them in years.

When I put myself out there
I just end up back at the start
Because they reject me
And it destroys my heart.

But I feel like I'm in the wrong
So I stay away from people
I don't want to hurt them
Because I feel evil.

So I just keep to myself.
I let the problems dissolve
And I start to feel numb.
I just start to devolve.

In the midst of it all
I had a major loss.

Someone left me
And it got to my thoughts.

I felt horrible all the time
And never wanted to feel like this
Or anyone to feel so sick,
So I looked around and no one was in a bliss.

I start to realize
That people look like me
And they are miserable
Now that's all I see.

So I start to listen again.
And they all have different things to say.
And I want to hear them out,
So I decide to stay.

The more that I focused
I noticed all the misery,
I saw,
That we are not all simplicity.

So I decided not to brush people off
And look at everyone's position.
So I let other people talk
That's why I started to listen.

There Is a Sunflower in My Heart

Avery Molm

My grandma always said that I have a loving heart,
That if I saw a person in need, I would do anything to
    help them.
I feel like that is what sets me apart.
In the world we live in today,
I feel like we need a ray
Of sunshine cast upon us
To make us realize that there is something more
Than nameless fighting,
Something more than war and today's "society"
Making us second guess ourselves.
In the world we live in today,
We need a ray
Of sunshine cast upon us.

Overthinking

Haley Pearson

I think overthinking is like a drug.
Once you start to do it
The more you do it
The more it is harder to stop.

Hi, I'm Haley.
I am an overthinker.
I overthink a lot of situations.
Overthinking kinda stresses me out.
I overthink about school, friends, or relationships.
I overthink about if my friends are good for me, or if
   they are a bad person.
I overthink if I'm doing good or terrible in school.
I overthink about my relationship with someone, like
   if they are treating me right or if I should end
   things.
When I overthink, it's like me asking so many
   questions that aren't needed.
When I overthink, it's like I need answers or I stress out.

Stress makes you go crazy.
You feel under threat.

Overthinking can last days.
You just keep thinking it over and over.

You keep thinking about what you did wrong or what
   you could have done.
Sometimes you blame the stuff that happened
   on yourself.
Overthinking is like depression and it makes you
   feel down.
Sometimes nothing happens and you still think you
   did something wrong.

Overthinking makes me cry.
Thinking I did something wrong or I'm losing someone.
I hate losing people.
Overthinking just makes me think about things
   that probably
Would never happen.
Everyone overthinks about some situations.
Some people have it worse than most.

Overthinking is very hard to get over.
People say just don't overthink.
It isn't that easy to just stop.
The reason why most people overthink is because they
   lost someone for not thinking about something.
So they overthink.
They don't try to but it just happens.
You think of all the good things that could happen
   and the bad things.

Caring

Haley Pearson

I am a very caring person.
I worry about a lot of people.
Caring comes naturally.
I care for everyone,
Even when I don't know them.

I care so much that I hide my feelings.
Rather, I care about other people more than myself.
I usually get other people's problems and help
    them out.
Then after I'm done helping them, I help myself.

Hiding your feelings is a very bad thing.
It is like a drug.
Once you take it, you don't stop.
I want to have everyone be happy before
    I am happy.
I care so much that I sometimes feel the way
    the other person feels.

The way I care about people kinda sounds
    depressing.
To me it is just me really wanted my friend
    to be happy.
I do care about myself and everything.
But my mom helps me out.

So I help my friends and they help me.
That's kinda how it works I guess.

My friends mean more than anything to me.
So, I try to make them smile and feel better.
I will be there for them no matter what.
I do the same thing with my family.
All the people in my life are the reason I am happy.
They make me smile.
So, when they are down or something
I will be there to make them smile,
To make their day.

I feel like everyone deserves to be happy.
Little things can make a person happy.
Money doesn't make anyone happy,
But them realizing that someone cares.
It seriously will make someone's day.

Family

Haley Pearson

Someone I think of as family is Skarlett.
Ever since I met her she has been there since day one.
She has all my trust.
She doesn't realize how amazing she is.
She brightens my day with her beautiful smile.
She makes me laugh.
Her words are true and meaningful.
She is very outgoing.
She will seriously do anything to make you happy.
She is very loving.
She cares about you.
She sticks by your side.
She is real and true.
She is one like no other.
She will take a bullet for you.
She will go through all this pain for you to be happy.
She is the strongest person I have met.
She is as beautiful as a flower garden.
Her personality is special.
Our friendship is like two peas in a pot.

Skarlett is like a sister I never had.
I mean I have two sisters, but this relationship
    is different.
We are the friends meant to be.

Our friendship is like the one friendship
  everyone wants.
She is the person I absolutely don't want to lose.
She is a very special person.
She doesn't realize how much she means to me,
But she really means the world.
She actually deserves the world, more than
  anyone does.
She is like a walking angel on Earth.
Once you are her friend and you leave...
You are going to want her back cause you are gonna
  miss her personality.
Her love and sweetness are what makes her
  so amazing.

Identity

Bette Schmieding

I'm from a small town.
A town built on the dust kicked up from
    workers' boots,
A town built on years of labor and memories,
A town built on farmland passed on from
    father to son,
A town built on progress.

I'm from the Southside.
A neighborhood built on community,
A neighborhood built on poverty,
A neighborhood built on humble upbringings,
A neighborhood built on stigma.

I'm from a large family.
A family built on love,
A family built on shared recipes,
A family built on generations of stories,
A family built on acceptance.

I'm me
I'm built on family,
I'm built on love,
I'm built on humble upbringings,
I'm me.

Her

Bette Schmieding

I met you again today—
There you stood in front of me,
Just as beautiful as I remember.
Your hair as blonde as the sun,
Your eyes as blue as the most valuable sapphire,
But something was off.
It was something about who you were,
You just weren't you.
Maybe it was the happiness in your eyes.
Maybe it was the spring in your step.
You seemed like a shell of who you were.
I'm not sure what it was, but something in you
    was gone.
I miss the person you were before they sent
    you away.
But I still love you.
Damn, do I love you.
And I know you're still in there.
So until we meet again in some random encounter,
All I can hope is that you'll be yourself and you didn't
    let them change you.

The Tree on the Hill

Bette Schmieding

There's a path in the grass that leads to the
    melancholy tree on the hill.
A path paved with the names of everyone
    you knew.
And even though their names are there, you'll walk
    that path alone.
On that path the air seems heavy and the sound of
    voices are drowned out
by the defining white noise of tv static and the
    haunting hum of fluorescent lights.
You'll walk that path to the tree and gaze at the grass
    along your side—
it's always greener where you're not.
You'll walk that path with a shameless stride until you
    fall to your knees
at the base of that melancholy tree.
There at the base, all of the white noise will silence
and you'll hear the sound of voices.
Voices of everything you knew,
The sweet melody of your favorite song,
Your favorite story told by your favorite person,
The script of your favorite episode of your
    favorite show.
And in that moment, all will be at peace.

Then you'll pick up that rope made of your
 wrongdoings
and you'll hang from that melancholy tree.
One day we'll all hang from that melancholy tree.

Kind of Girl

Alexia Woolsey

I am a rough-and-tumble kind of girl
I grew up listening to rock
On those hundred-degree mornings
In the garage with my dad
Learning how to reload and make bullets
I learned how to shoot before I could ride a bike,
I am used to being covered in dirt and grime
I am not afraid to get my hands dirty
I want to fix things
I am an artistic kind of girl
Paint covered hands
Muddy paint water
Sketchbooks half-finished
Humid nights spent drawing up a new idea
Constantly taking photographs
Makes colorful collages out of anything
I could get my hands on
I want to create
I am a writing kind of girl
Hundreds of stories created
But not finished
Goals not yet met
But I'm working on it
Coffee and staying up well past the sunset

Tired eyes but a hungry mind
I read hundreds of books in a span of a few months
Gathering and hoarding ideas
Like a book dragon,
Waiting to unleash my fury of a story
Eventually
I am fragile kind of girl
Mind as unstable as the universe
Nights spent crying
To no one but myself
The feeling of emptiness made its home in me
Nothing could make me change
Barely any motivation to live
Or to fight
I still try, and there's success in that
But there will come a time when
I will break

I am a warrior kind of girl
Despite my hardships,
The friendships which I cannot form
The relationships which I cannot hold
I still live
I am so strong,
To live day after day,
No matter how hard it is
No matter how rough my mind comes
As choppy and as harsh as the waves guarding the
coast,

And as destructive as a forest fire
Yet as an ocean is,
I am filled with life
As a fire is,
I will be rekindled
I may collapse
I may crumble
But I always remember
This is not the end
I am a hardworking kind of girl
If it's not working and I feel frustrated
I come back later
I let myself come back with
New ideas, new theories
Try again,
And again
Until success
Because nothing was ever perfect
The first time it was done
I will try again
I am a rough-and-tumble kind of girl
I go hunting with my dad,
I fist fight with my bad memories
I rebuild myself constantly
I may collapse
But I always get back up
I am rough, shards of broken glass
I am tumble, scars on my arms
I am a warrior,

I don't care what others say
I have my own goals
I know what I want
And I'm gonna get it
Because that is who I am

Cali Girl / Montana Girl

Alexia Woolsey

I am the Cali girl,
Raised in California
For more than a decade of my life
I was the loner girl,
The book worm
Rather read than discuss with the class
Rather sit by myself
Than interact with anyone at all
I was the rough kid,
Always got into fights
Always got into trouble
And trouble found me

I am the Montana girl,
Raised in Montana
For more than a year of my life
I am the friendly girl
The good kid
Rather work ahead of time then do it later
Rather be with my friends
Than be stuck all alone
I am the rough kid,
Always looking out for people
Always getting into trouble because of it
Because I found trouble

DENI OLTROGGE
Billings Career Center

9th Grade English Period 3

My Name

Leslie Abrahams

My name is something I hear every day
Just like the sound of the sirens
My name is personal to my family
Just like the relationship of two best friends
My name has a meaning behind it
Just like it did to the girl once before
Even though she is no longer here
The name Leslie will always be special to me

I See Her There

Ruth Adams

I see her there
Making my sister and I breakfast in the early morning,
the warm smell of the chorizo, eggs, and sausage.
Trying to see more of what she's doing as I'm still
   trying to wake up.
Seeing her hair long and dark through the morning
   sun's summer glare.
I can see her wondering when her two
   granddaughters will wake up
and enjoy the meal she made.
      I can see my sister doing the same thing as me.
Through the window left of me, opened by a sliver,
I hear the birds' music and the cicadas' humming for
   the little city to hear.
The wind moves through the trees creating the
   softest little whisper,
Only to be interrupted by the growling of my stomach,
telling me that it's time to get up.

Swing High, Swing Low

Haley Adams

As the wind flows through her hair
Her legs swing back and forth.

As the leafy trees move with the wind
Her legs swing back and forth.

As the leaves dance around her legs
Her legs swing back and forth.

As the light from the sun beams
Her legs swing back and forth.

As the leaves dance on her legs.
She swings high.
She swings low.

Olivia

From the Latin Origin of Olive Trees

Olivia Bronson

They're short and majestic.
Cracks appear as life goes on,
but with longevity
they always succeed.

Both produce bitterness,
but create better versions of themselves.
After going through crackling fires
and important life lessons
they always come back
brighter than the sun.

Social butterflies,
they both take roots easily.
When finding their comfort zones
they reach out fast while stopping
many times at puddles and tears
along the way.

As seasons change with beautiful
embellishments starting to appear,
draping of foliage gives them assurance.
Through their oils they supply enrichment,
comfort, and loyalty, that encompasses those close.

Locals call them Ελιά Βουβών "heyovendro."
They also will be remembered as Olivia,
the short and majestic that always succeed.

The Third Weekend of August

Nashantee Deputee

I see vibrant colors all around me.
I hear jingles, the sound of the drums going boom
boom boom,
singing in native tongue,
the powwow manager directing the dancers,
and laughter from joyful youngsters and elders
The drums going boom boom boom
is a familiar sound I love to hear during
this time of year

In my earlier years I use to be one of the dancers
My mother would help me put on
my gorgeous regalia
Because I had so much energy, I was fit to be a jingle
dress dancer
My regalia jingled with every step and sparkled and
shined in daylight
I always felt proud when I got to put on my beautiful
dress
to show off and impress

Reminiscing on the more exciting times of Crow Fair
when I was a tyke,
I wonder what it might be like when I
become an elder
Will the area expand?

166

Will I have my own campground
knowing that many places people camp at
are reserved?
Or will Crow Fair be exciting as ever to dream about
forever?

Now I know I tend to forget a lot,
but I hope I'll be able to remember my time
as a youngster
I don't want to forget these treasuring memories
I want to pass down my memories
and to tell my stories of exciting events I've
experienced to my grandchildren one day who will
hopefully pass down to their children

My Sisters Are Food

Nashantee Deputee

They can be tasteful but other times awful
They smell like mold just like the cold
Like a waffle, how yawn-full

Other times they are sweet
Tasting quite like a treat
But don't get too friendly
For they are deadly

When they are spicy
They get pricey

The Thoughts Before Exciting News

Nashantee Deputee

No, I will not feel enclosed
I will not let it hold me back and keep me from
pursuing my goals
Have confidence and be strong is what everyone
keeps telling me
People are going to support me and have my back
so why do I feel so scared

Couple more days now
I need to get these posters done
I need to finish and they must look amazing

Thank goodness I had help and the posters are way
better than I expected
But now I need to figure out how I want to represent
myself to others
Ok, I just told friends to vote! It sounds like I have
promising voters
Now all I have to do is wait patiently
Oh no! What if all my hard work is for nothing and I
don't get any positions

I guess I will hear the results 5th period
I feel so nervous and scared

Wait! The girl's locker room is so loud, and I missed
   the announcements!
OK, I will take some friends with me to go find out
   from the office
I'm feeling nauseous and this rushing is killing me
Now I have to go upstairs to find out

Ready? I open the closed door to a room full of the
   student body seniors
I ask them if they know who had won
   freshman president
They respond with the name of Nashantee Deputee

I can't express how delighted I felt
I wanted to cry I was so happy
My friends are amazing!
This day is the best day ever!!!!

Going Home

Breklen Draayer

The sweet smell of maple syrup
Beautiful bright blue eyes just like the color of the ocean
She had light brown hair with warm caramel highlights
Her contagious giggle rings in my ears like big red bells
The breeze was chilly and light
The sun was big and bright
Laying on our backs on a big black blanket
Making pictures out the clouds
She asked me if we could go fly
I told her it wasn't her time yet
But god knew she was more than ready
And he took her home

My Family is the Earth

Skylar Kennedy

My family is the
earth
My mom is the
gravity keeping us down to earth managing
  each moment
My papa is the
topography giving life variety
My sisters are the
ocean, constantly crashing making noise
I am the
moon causing the waves
My dad is the
wise owl always guiding my path of life.
Our house is the
galaxy that we all live in

My German Great Grandma

Alyssa Rambur

I can see her
Sitting in her old corduroy chair
Up by the counter talking
To my great grandpa sitting next to her
In an identical chair
With Sammie
The Shih Tzu always by his feet
Never leaving his side
Watching the small tv
With the news always on
The candy on the counter to the one side
With the mail and papers to the other side
The smell of mint and caramel in the air
Thinking of her days owning the Dairy Queen
All the kids she would get to see
Or maybe thinking of the next meal she might cook
Like the delicious German meals
She would make the best
Fleischkuekle
It was so filling
With the taste of
Fried dough and hamburger
That would make us sleep
Sleep so good at night

Smith, Fire, and Us

Brennen Sunderland

It's late, fire is dying, trees are swaying lightly
in the breeze.
He's sitting in his chair, tired, but awake.
We look across the fire, she stares back.
We talk for hours, we add another log.
We dive deep into the meaning of life.
The long day of rowing has us completely open to
each other in the late hours.
Secrets we swear to die with don't seem so bad
in the fire's light.
Life, problems, soreness and pain drift away.
Next to the fire, in the night, with him.

Boundaries

Brennen Sunderland

I am 4, i can't start school yet
I am bound by age, all i want is to be old enough
I am 12, i'm not in middle school yet
I am bound by my grade, all i want is to be older
I am 13, but i'm not in high school yet,
I am again bound by my grade, all i want is to be old
    enough
I am 14, but i cannot drive yet
I am bound by my parents, all i want is to be
    old enough,
I am 15, but i cannot join the military and leave home
    yet
I am bound by the law, all i want is to be
    old enough
I am 16, but i am still in high school
I am bound by time, all i want is to be old enough
I am 17 but i cannot be my own man
I am bound by my age, all i want is to be
    old enough
I am 18, but i cannot move out yet,
I am bound by money, all i want is to be old enough
I am 25, i can do anything i want,
I am only bound by the law i am old enough,
I am now 50 i am my own man,

I am bound by myself, i wish i was young enough.
I am 60, but i cannot live alone,
I am bound by the people in my house, i wish i was
    young enough
I am 70, but i cannot walk by myself,
I am bound by my walker, i wish i was
    young enough.
I am 94, but i cannot leave my hospital bed
I am bound by the hospital staff i wish i was
    young enough
I have passed on now, i cannot do anything
I am bound by death, i wish i had more time

The Wall

Brennen Sunderland

In front of me there is a 9-foot wall
To my left is a man, yelling, telling me to get over
   that wall
I look at the wall thinking, "I can't."
The man in a smoky hat says I will, now a second man
   joins him
I run at the wall placing my left foot against it firmly.
I push up off my foot with all my power
And fall back to the ground.
When I land, I look up and see now three men
   standing over me.
They yell all at different times
"GET UP THAT WALL!"
And prepare a second time knowing that this time I
   can do it!
And run again this time placing my right foot on
   the wall
Again, I land on my back. BOOM
As I slowly get up, the final two men join the other
   three. I am surrounded
They tell me this is my last chance.
I run as hard as I can, jumping off my left foot again.
I threw my arms up, hoping I'll grab the top of the
   wall.

But I don't, I fall back to the ground
But before I hit the ground I stop.
There is now another man sitting on top of the wall
   holding my hand.
He helps me up and over.
When we hit the ground, the five men form before
   . are yelling
They tell us "GET IN THE SAND PIT!!!"
We sprint to the pit and dive in
Immediately we begin with pushups sit ups and
   anything else you can imagine
During this I look at the man who helped me,
He notices my apologetic face
And smiles

I See Him There

Cayden Thornock

I see him there
Standing on the beach with the waves washing onto
his feet
Sand getting in between his toes
He runs into the water jumps in and shrieks of
coldness
He runs out of the water as he sees his friends
standing there laughing at him
I see him there he is running onto a professional
major league baseball field
He runs around the bases as he hits a home run
I see him there as he runs onto a soccer field he kicks
the ball and scores a goal
I see him there he rides his bike into a skatepark he
does some tricks

Where I Am From

Brenna Townsend

I am from where land meets the sky
I am from where the western meadowlarks always fly
I am from where—every year—the snow falls
     It glitters blues and pinks as the sun shines on it,
     Lightly drifting down to the ground
I am from where we answer when nature calls
I am from where lakes are goldfields of bitterroot
I am from where dirt gets tracked in from fields
  of tall grasses
      And overgrown tree roots
I am from where a gentle breeze blows
I am from where it gets thirty-five below when it snows
     Blowing down into the valleys below
I am from where, on the ranch, we wear
  cowboy boots
I am from where no one ever wears suits
I am from where there are wide, open plains
     High, rolling land and wide river valleys
I am from where, when I ride across the grasslands
     And dirt roads, horses have reins
I am from where there are always beautiful sunsets
     Reds, pinks, and purples above
       the mountains
I am from where the rest of the world forgets

I am from where ranchers and coal miners work hard
I am from where kids run and yell in the front yard
I am from where we play and watch many sports
    Softball, soccer, and track in the
      warm weather
I am from where, in the summer, all but ranchers and
  cattlemen wear shorts
I am from where, when we are in the tall grasses, we
  must be careful
    Snakes coiled-up, holes hidden, as well as
      newborn meadowlarks nesting
I am from where teenagers are playing on rims. . .
  always dareful
    Standing, toes on the edge, looking out over
      the town
I am from where horses roam through the grasslands,
  coulees and plains
    Running to feel the wind across their face and
      through their mane
I am from where everyone in this state
  always remains.

Our Favorite Place

Brenna Townsend

I can see him there
Sitting on the grass-covered bank
Wearing jeans, plain t-shirts, tennis shoes and a hat
At our favorite spot, the lake just a few minutes from
  our house
Waiting for a fish to come by in a humid 96 degrees
Listening to the birds and watching the ripples in
  the water
Suddenly, there is a bite on the line
He starts to reel it in, we hope we don't lose it
We knew it wasn't gonna be big since we were at the
  small lake
And was going to get thrown back, like we always do
But we wanted to know what we caught
Once it was out of the water and brought closer
  to us
We saw that it was a bright yellow Bream
The Bream was smaller than his whole hand
It was shining in the sun from the water
I slowly removed the hook from its mouth while he
  held it
We tossed it back into the water and cast out again
My father and I sat on the bank all day

La Familia

Chasity Trujillo

Warm and pleasant,
Kind and caring,
How are they faring?

Screaming and shattering,
A chain that's rusted and cracking,
Splitting away from one another.

Lost and unfound,
A never-ending race just to survive.

They are not proud,
Untrusting and furious,
A darker energy they emit.

They all have knives in their backs,
Tears rolling down their cheeks,
Betrayal and deceit all exposed for the world to see.

Sirens are blaring,
Glass is breaking,
Their screams are bouncing off the walls.

Fighting mixed with mockery,
Whose fault is it?

They are all looking for someone to blame,
They can't seem to get along the same.
Broken down stones being crushed by the waves,

Heart breaks and losses,
They'll keep it all in a locket
And just hide it away in their pocket.

Bittersweet Mistakes

Chasity Trujillo

Sharp burning,
Knocked down by my own hand,
A chuckle, laughter,
Maybe I was never the smart one?

Perhaps, I should listen more,
Sit and pay attention more,
Stare at a wall,
Trained to focus.

No, no,
The mirror betrays me again,
Risen only to fall,
Slamming against the wall,
Screaming and shouting,
At least he couldn't hear.

I stayed silent,
So did he,
So now he'll never know how moronic I felt

It was laughable,
Enjoyable,
That burning feeling as i berated myself.
Was I betraying myself?

Loopy, unaware,
What time was it?
What day was it?
Minutes, hours, days, years…

The dead lights flickering ever few,
The moonlight shining through that stained window,
The heat pressed against my back,

Peaceful tranquility at last.

Tranquility, what is tranquility?
Hyped, extreme breathing,
Bumping, bumping, bumping,
Slapping and punching,

Disconnected, too far gone,
Here, there, nowhere,
Sudden silence, a cease of tears…

Rising, stumbling,
Listening to the creak of the opening door.
He wasn't back yet,
He didn't care.

Perhaps I'll just lay down
And try to forget.
But will he let me?

A Mirror's Tale

Chasity Trujillo

When I look into the mirror, I see myself,
I feel upset and unimportant,
I wonder how life could be different and what the
   day will look like.
When I look into the mirror, I see myself, feel upset
   and unimportant,
I wonder how things will be and how they
   could've been,
But that is not
True,
Because I am important,
I belong,
And I hope nothing could change.

When I look into the mirror, I see myself,
Wonder why I'm upset and unimportant,
What could be different if I never made mistakes,
Wonder who I'm looking at,
Who is the stranger in the mirror?

When I look in the mirror,
I see myself,
Disconnected and confused,

Feeling as if I was a lion in a zoo,
But that is not
True.

When I look in the mirror,
I see myself.

The Wolf

Will Wegner

The Wolf
Travels through the wood
On a midnight hunt
Searching for his next meal

His coat is stained red and brown
From the mud and blood
But yet the snow around him stays white
As if a fresh fleet has sparkled to the
Ground.

He is in search of his brothers
As they have carved their own path
In this unforgiving wilderness
That they call home…

Many of the same animals are around him
Like the fox
Searching for the mouse that's hidden under
The hard, snow packed ground.

Or the elk
Proud and tall as he eats
The individual pine
Needles
That sprinkle the hardened
Conifers…

For winter has been hard on them all...

But continues the wolf
As it travels through the wood
Crunching the snow at his feet
With every single paw

On the same midnight hunt
With the same mud and blood
Stained coat.
He continues.

He Remembers

Will Wegner

He remembers
That November
Its taste still
Burns on his tongue.

His grandpas glass jar
Could have brought him
So far...
But what has he become?

If you want it
He can get it.
Just check your
Yard in a night or two.

He's got judges
In his pocket
For they get
Thirsty too

For that good old
Copper water
From pipes that line the hill
Sparkling bronze in the
Sunbaked dirt.

He hears the fizz
And the buzz
It hits the funnel
He hears sirens
And shouts
Dogs barking
Cars revving
"They're probably coming"

For some might call it evil
Or illegal

But the pride and fear
Still drives him near
Because it's in his blood to
Shine.

And that's what he would do to
Survive.

Fun at First

Haley Wine

I was 8 when a life-changing event happened.
It started as a game.
First it was fine, then it happened,
It went from laughing to panicking.
It went from hide and seek to a hospital visit, and
Talking to the police,
Him going to jail.
Why was this happening to me?
What was happening?

Memories

Haley Wine

1 cut, 2 cuts
Now there's 10
Each one is a lash out at a person, at a memory i
   wanna forget
Some are long like a river; others are small
   like a stream.
With each one it brings a memory back
Seeing him, talking to him, letting him
hurt me emotionally over and over again
Having it play over and over again in my head,
   thinking it was my fault
Not good memories, ones full of hurt, pain,
   and anger
Talking causes vulnerability, opening causes pain
10 minutes turn into an hour when talking
Tears start to drop as the pain pours out and the
   memories come back
From counselor to therapist to now all the
   people close
But they're all a cry for help
Help with the stress
Help with the pain
And most of all help forgetting the memories that
   need to be forgotten

Each one reminds me of how i failed, it wasn't
   my fault
but i could have stopped it

Heart Butte, Montana

by M. L. Smoker

The unsympathetic wind, how she has evaded me for
years now,
leaving a guileless shell and no way to
navigate. Once when I stood on a plateau of earth
just at the moment before the dangerous, jutting
peaks converged upon the sway of grasslands, I
almost found a way back. There, the sky, quite
possibly all the elements,
caused the rock and soil and vegetation to
congregate. Their prayer was not new and so faint I
could hardly discern. Simple remembrances, like a
tiny, syncopated chorus calling everyone
home: across a thousand eastward miles. And what
little wind was left at my back.
I could not move and then the music was gone.
All that was left were the springtime faces of
mountains, gazing down, their last patches of snow,
luminous. I dreamed of becoming snow melt,
gliding down the slope of history and into the
valley. With the promise,
an assurance, that there is always a way to become
bird, tree, water again.

Made in the USA
Middletown, DE
16 May 2021

39095420R00128